Ceremony of Psalms

David Willcocks

for baritone solo, chorus, and orchestra

Vocal Score

Music Department
OXFORD UNIVERSITY PRESS
Oxford and New York

Oxford University Press, Walton Street, Oxford OX2 6DP, England
Oxford University Press, 200 Madison Avenue, New York, NY 10016, USA

Oxford is a trade mark of Oxford University Press

The three choral movements (1, 3, and 5) may be performed as separate anthems,
and each is available separately. The accompaniment in this vocal score is therefore
written for organ. The two solo movements are given with a piano reduction
of the orchestral accompaniment.

Permission to perform this work in public (except in the course of divine worship) should
normally be obtained from the Performing Rights Society Ltd. (PRS), 29/33 Berners Street,
London W1P 4AA, or its affiliated Societies in each country throughout the world, unless the
owner or the occupier of the premises being used holds a licence from the Society.

Permission to make a recording must be obtained in advance from the Mechanical Copyright
Protection Society Ltd. (MCPS), Elgar House, 41 Streatham High Road, London SW16 1ER,
or its affiliated Societies in each country throughout the world.

Ceremony of Psalms was composed in 1989 in response to an invitation from the Green Lake (Wisconsin) Festival of Music to write a work for baritone solo, chorus, and orchestra to mark the tenth anniversary of the founding of the Festival.

The verbal text was selected from the Book of Psalms, a collection of 150 Hebrew religious poems which were sung in the worship of the Temple in Jerusalem. The five psalms reflect the emotional range of these poems, for they voice joy and sorrow, thanksgiving and despair, penitence and faith, hope and love.

Psalm 98 is a song of praise to Jehovah for the redemption of Israel and a call to all humans and to all nature to rejoice at his coming to judge the earth.
Psalm 130 is a cry to God from the depths for pardon. Confident of forgiveness, the Psalmist waits for God and bids Israel to wait for redemption.
Psalm 150 exhorts all living creatures to recognize the majesty of God and to praise God through music.
Psalm 23 is a personal expression of trust in God, the true shepherd, who will guide and sustain through life and death.
Psalm 65 is a hymn of praise, probably intended to be sung at the presentation of the first-fruits at the Passover. It is a thanksgiving to God for his mercy despite human sin, and a confident proclamation that, in the future as in the past, God will defend his people and provide for them bountiful harvests.

David Willcocks

The first complete performance of Ceremony of Psalms was given on 29 July 1989 at the Music Hall, Arts and Communication Centre, University of Wisconsin-Oshkosh, as part of the Green Lake Festival of Music. Sir David Willcocks conducted the Green Lake Festival Chorus and Orchestra, with Douglas Morris, baritone.

Orchestra

2 flutes	4 horns (ad lib)	timpani
2 oboes	3 trumpets	percussion
2 clarinets (ad lib)	3 trombones (ad lib)	
2 bassoons	1 tuba (ad lib)	strings

Text from Book of Common Prayer

I

Psalm 98 (for chorus and orchestra)

O sing unto the Lord a new song: for he hath done marvellous things.
With his own right hand, and with his holy arm: hath he gotten himself the victory.
The Lord declared his salvation: his righteousness hath he openly shewed in the sight of the heathen.
He hath remembered his mercy and truth toward the house of Israel: and all the ends of the world have seen the salvation of our God.
Shew yourselves joyful unto the Lord, all ye lands: sing, rejoice, and give thanks.
Praise the Lord upon the harp: sing to the harp with a psalm of thanksgiving.
With trumpets also, and shawms: O shew yourselves joyful before the Lord the King.
Let the sea make a noise, and all that therein is: the round world and they that dwell therein.
Let the floods clap their hands, and let the hills be joyful together before the Lord: for he is come to judge the earth.
With righteousness shall he judge the world: and the people with equity.
Glory be to the Father, and to the Son: and to the Holy Ghost;
As it was in the beginning, is now and ever shall be: world without end. Amen.

II

Psalm 130 (for baritone solo and orchestra)

Out of the deep have I called unto thee O Lord: Lord hear my voice.
O let thine ears consider well: the voice of my complaint.
If thou Lord wilt be extreme to mark what is done amiss: O Lord who may abide it?
For there is mercy with thee: therefore shalt thou be feared.
I look for the Lord, my soul doth wait for him: in his word is my trust.
My soul fleeth unto the Lord: before the morning watch, I say before the morning watch.
O Israel trust in the Lord, for with the Lord there is mercy: and with him is plenteous redemption.
And he shall redeem Israel: from all his sins.

III

Psalm 150 (for chorus and orchestra)

O praise God in his holiness: praise him in the firmament of his power.
Praise him in his noble acts: praise him according to his excellent greatness.
Praise him in the sound of the trumpet: praise him upon the lute and harp.
Praise him in the cymbals and dances: praise him upon the strings and pipe.
Praise him upon the well-tuned cymbals: praise him upon the loud cymbals.
Let everything that hath breath: praise the Lord.

IV

Psalm 23 (for baritone solo and orchestra)

The Lord is my shepherd: therefore can I lack nothing.
He shall feed me in a green pasture: and lead me forth beside the waters of comfort.
He shall convert my soul: and bring me forth in the paths of righteousness for his Name's sake.
Yea thou I walk through the valley of the shadow of death, I will fear no evil: for thou art with me,
thy rod and thy staff comfort me.
Thou shalt prepare a table before me, against them that trouble me: thou hast anointed my head with oil and my cup shall be full.
But thy loving kindness and mercy shall follow me, all the days of my life: and I will dwell in the house of the Lord for ever.

V

Psalm 65 (for chorus and orchestra)

Thou, O God, art praised in Sion: and unto thee shall the vow be performed in Jerusalem.
Thou that hearest the prayer: unto thee shall all flesh come.
My misdeeds prevail against me: O be thou merciful unto our sins.
Blessed is the man whom thou choosest, and receivest unto thee: he shall dwell in thy court, and shall be satisfied with the pleasures of thy house, even of thy holy temple.
Thou shalt shew us wonderful things in thy righteousness, O God of our salvation: thou that art the hope of all the ends of the earth, and of them that remain in the broad sea.
Who in his strength setteth fast the mountains: and is girded about with power.
Who stilleth the raging of the sea: and the noise of his waves, and the madness of the people.
They also that dwell in the uttermost parts of the earth shall be afraid at thy tokens: thou that makest the outgoings of the morning and evening to praise thee.
Thou visitest the earth and blessest it: thou makest it very plenteous.
The river of God is full of water: thou preparest their corn, for so thou providest for the earth.
Thou waterest her furrows, thou sendest rain into the little valleys thereof: thou makest it soft with the drops of rain, and blessest the increase of it.
Thou crownest the year with thy goodness: and thy clouds drop fatness.
They shall drop upon the dwellings of the wilderness: and the little hills shall rejoice on every side.
The folds shall be full of sheep: the valleys also shall stand so thick with corn that they shall laugh and sing.
Glory be to the Father, and to the Son: and to the Holy Ghost;
As it was in the beginning, is now and ever shall be: world without end. Amen.

Ceremony of Psalms

For Stanford and Phyllis Lehmberg in celebration of the 25th anniversary of their marriage

1. O sing unto the Lord a new song

Psalm 98

Book of Common Prayer

DAVID WILLCOCKS

4

O sing unto the Lord a new song

sing   to the harp   with a psalm of   thanks-giv-ing.

Praise___   the   Lord   up-on the   harp:___

O sing unto the Lord a new song

12

sing   to the harp with a psalm of thanks-giv - ing. ____

With trum-pets al - so, and shawms,   with trum-pets al - so, and

O sing unto the Lord a new song

O sing unto the Lord a new song

joy-ful be-fore___ the Lord the King,___ the Lord the King,___ the

Lord the King.

Let the

64

sea   make a noise, and all   that there-in   is: the

66

round world,   and they   that   dwell   there-in.

O sing unto the Lord a new song

for Douglas Morris

2. Out of the deep

Psalm 130

Book of Common Prayer

DAVID WILLCOCKS

© Oxford University Press 1993

Out of the deep

My soul fle – eth un – to the Lord: be – fore the morn – ing watch, I say, be – fore the morn – ing watch. _____ O Is – ra – el, trust in the Lord, for with the Lord there is mer – cy: and with him is plen – teous re – demp – tion. And

Out of the deep

he shall re-deem_ Is – ra-el:_____ from all his sins, and

he shall re-deem_ Is – ra-el:_____ from all his sins.

3. O praise God in his holiness

Psalm 150

Book of Common Prayer

DAVID WILLCOCKS

O praise God in his holiness

O praise God in his holiness

O praise God in his holiness

32

O praise God in his holiness

O praise God in his holiness

34

O praise God in his holiness

O praise God in his holiness

38

O praise God in his holiness

for Douglas Morris

4. The Lord is my shepherd

Psalm 23

Book of Common Prayer

DAVID WILLCOCKS

The Lord is my shepherd

31
-pare a ta- ble be-fore me____ a-gainst them that trou - ble me:

(p) f p

(loco)

33
thou hast an - oint - ed my head with oil, and my

f

cresc.

35
rall. a tempo

cup shall be full.

molto cresc. ff

38

fff ff

The Lord is my shepherd

42
f dim.
mf
mp
p
pp
47
p dolce ed espressivo
But thy lov - ing kind-ness and mer-cy shall fol-low me all the days of my life:
50
mp cresc.
mf
rit.
and I will dwell in the house of the Lord for ev - - - er, for
53
a tempo
p
ev - er, for ev - er.
Fl.
mp
Str.
pp
ppp niente

5. Thou, O God, art praised in Sion

Psalm 65

Book of Common Prayer

DAVID WILLCOCKS

45

Thou, O God, art praised in Sion

Thou, O God, art praised in Sion

Thou, O God, art praised in Sion

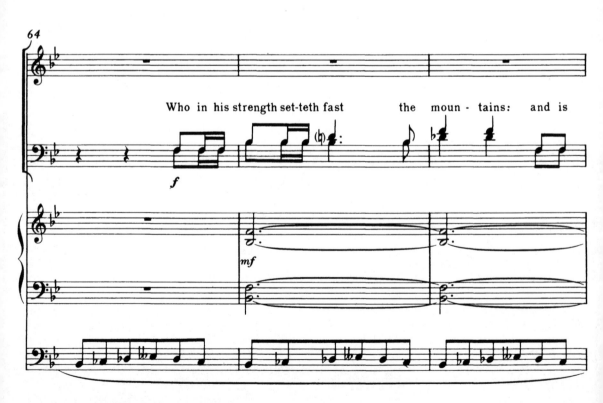

Thou, O God, art praised in Sion

Thou, O God, art praised in Sion

out - go-ings of the morn - ing and__ eve - ning to__

praise_____ thee, to praise_____ thee, to

praise_____ thee.

Thou, O God, art praised in Sion

Thou, O God, art praised in Sion

109 wa - ter-est her fur-rows, thou send - est rain in-to the lit - tle

111 val - leys there - of: thou mak-est it

113 soft with the drops of rain, and bless - est the in - crease of it.

Thou, O God, art praised in Sion

119

year with thy good-ness: and thy clouds drop fat - ness. They shall drop up - on the

and thy clouds drop fat - ness. They shall drop up - on the dwell - ings, the

121

dwell-ings of the wil - der-ness: and the lit - tle
the

dwell-ings of the wil - der-ness: and the lit - tle hills

mf

mf

Thou, O God, art praised in Sion

58

Thou, O God, art praised in Sion

Thou, O God, art praised in Sion